Mastering Large Language Models with PyTorch: A

Hands-On Guide with Practical Code Examples

# Table of Contents

## 4. Data Preparation

- Collecting and Preprocessing Text Data

- Tokenization

- Creating Datasets and DataLoaders in PyTorch

## 5. Building LLMs from Scratch

- Model Architecture

  - Embeddings

  - Attention Mechanism

  - Transformer Blocks

- Implementing the Model in PyTorch

  - Defining Layers

  - Forward Pass

## 6. Training Large Language Models

- Training Loop

# Introduction

*Overview of Large Language Models (LLMs)*

Large Language Models (LLMs) are advanced artificial intelligence systems designed to understand, generate, and manipulate human language. These models, often built using deep learning techniques, are capable of performing a wide range of tasks including translation, summarization, question answering, and text generation.

*Importance and Applications*

LLMs have transformed various industries by enabling:

- **Natural Language Processing (NLP)**: Improving chatbots, virtual assistants, and customer service.

- **Content Creation**: Assisting in writing articles, creating marketing content, and generating code.

- **Healthcare**: Analyzing patient records and assisting in medical research.

- **Education**: Providing personalized tutoring and generating educational content.

- **Finance**: Analyzing financial reports, predicting market trends, and automating trading strategies.

*Why PyTorch?*

PyTorch is a powerful, flexible deep learning framework favored for its dynamic computational graph and ease of use. It supports rapid prototyping and offers extensive libraries and tools, making it ideal for research and production-level model deployment.

**Getting Started with PyTorch**

*Installing PyTorch*

To install PyTorch, you can use pip (Python's package installer). Choose the correct version based on your operating system, CUDA (GPU support), and Python version. Here's a basic installation command for a CPU-only version:

bash

Copy code

```
pip install torch torchvision torchaudio
```

For a GPU-enabled installation (assuming CUDA is installed), you might use:

bash

Copy code

```
pip install torch torchvision torchaudio --extra-index-url https://download.pytorch.org/whl/cu113
```

## Setting Up the Environment

1. **Creating a Virtual Environment**:

   bash

   Copy code

   ```
   python -m venv pytorch_env
   source pytorch_env/bin/activate   # On Windows,
   use `pytorch_env\Scripts\activate`
   ```

2. **Installing Necessary Packages**:

   bash

   Copy code

   ```
   pip install torch torchvision torchaudio
   pip install jupyterlab matplotlib
   ```

3. **Starting JupyterLab**:

bash

Copy code

jupyter lab

*Basic Operations in PyTorch*

1. **Tensors**: The core data structure in PyTorch.

python

Copy code

```
import torch


# Creating a tensor

x = torch.tensor([[1, 2], [3, 4]])

print(x)
```

```python
# Basic operations
y = torch.ones_like(x)
z = x + y
print(z)
```

2. **Autograd**: Automatic differentiation for building and training neural networks.

python

Copy code

```python
# Creating a tensor with gradient tracking
a = torch.tensor([2.0, 3.0], requires_grad=True)
b = a ** 2
b.backward(torch.tensor([1.0, 1.0]))  # Backpropagation
```

```python
print(a.grad)  # Gradient of a
```

3. **Neural Networks**: Building simple neural networks using torch.nn.

python

Copy code

```python
import torch.nn as nn


# Simple linear model
model = nn.Linear(2, 1)
input = torch.tensor([[1.0, 2.0]])
output = model(input)
print(output)
```

**Understanding Large Language Models**

*What are LLMs?*

Large Language Models (LLMs) are neural networks with a vast number of parameters (typically in the billions) trained on massive corpora of text data. They are designed to understand and generate human language, exhibiting capabilities like contextual understanding, coherence in text generation, and the ability to transfer knowledge across tasks.

*Key Concepts and Terminology*

- **Tokenization**: The process of converting text into tokens (words, subwords, or characters) that the model can process.

- **Attention Mechanism**: A method that allows the model to focus on relevant parts of the input sequence when generating each part of the output.

- **Transformer Architecture**: A deep learning model architecture that relies heavily on self-attention mechanisms, foundational for most LLMs.

- **Pretraining and Fine-Tuning**: Pretraining on a large dataset to learn general language features, followed by fine-tuning on a specific task to specialize the model.

*Differences Between Various LLM Architectures*

- **GPT (Generative Pretrained Transformer)**: Focuses on text generation, using a unidirectional approach where each token is generated sequentially.

python

Copy code

```
from transformers import GPT2LMHeadModel,
GPT2Tokenizer


model_name = 'gpt2'
tokenizer =
GPT2Tokenizer.from_pretrained(model_name)
model =
GPT2LMHeadModel.from_pretrained(model_nam
e)
```

```python
input_text = "Once upon a time"

inputs = tokenizer(input_text, return_tensors='pt')

outputs = model.generate(inputs['input_ids'],

max_length=50)

print(tokenizer.decode(outputs[0],

skip_special_tokens=True))
```

- **BERT (Bidirectional Encoder Representations from Transformers)**: Designed for understanding and encoding text, using a bidirectional approach for contextual comprehension.

python

Copy code

```python
from transformers import BertTokenizer,

BertModel
```

```python
model_name = 'bert-base-uncased'

tokenizer =
BertTokenizer.from_pretrained(model_name)

model = BertModel.from_pretrained(model_name)


input_text = "Hello, my dog is cute"

inputs = tokenizer(input_text, return_tensors='pt')

outputs = model(**inputs)

print(outputs.last_hidden_state)
```

- **T5 (Text-To-Text Transfer Transformer):** Treats all
  NLP tasks as text-to-text problems, making it
  highly versatile.

  python

Copy code

```python
from transformers import T5Tokenizer,
T5ForConditionalGeneration


model_name = 't5-small'
tokenizer =
T5Tokenizer.from_pretrained(model_name)
model =
T5ForConditionalGeneration.from_pretrained(mo
del_name)


input_text = "translate English to French: The
house is wonderful."
inputs = tokenizer(input_text, return_tensors='pt')
```

```
outputs = model.generate(inputs['input_ids'],

max_length=50)

print(tokenizer.decode(outputs[0],

skip_special_tokens=True))
```

These code snippets and explanations provide a starting point for understanding and working with large language models in PyTorch. The hands-on examples demonstrate how to install PyTorch, create and manipulate tensors, build basic neural networks, and work with popular LLM architectures using the Hugging Face Transformers library.

**Data Preparation**

*Collecting and Preprocessing Text Data*

Data preparation is a crucial step in training LLMs. High-quality, diverse datasets are essential for building robust models.

1. **Collecting Data**:

   ○ **Public Datasets**: Use existing datasets like Wikipedia, Common Crawl, or specific NLP datasets from sources like Kaggle or Hugging Face Datasets.

   ○ **Web Scraping**: Collect data from websites using tools like BeautifulSoup or Scrapy, ensuring compliance with web scraping policies and copyright laws.

2. **Preprocessing Data**:

- ○ **Cleaning Text**: Remove unwanted characters, HTML tags, and other noise.

- ○ **Tokenization**: Convert text into tokens using libraries like Hugging Face's tokenizers or NLTK.

- ○ **Normalizing Text**: Convert text to lowercase, handle contractions, and standardize formats.

python

Copy code

```
from transformers import BertTokenizer


tokenizer = BertTokenizer.from_pretrained('bert-base-uncased')
```

```python
def preprocess_text(text):

    # Basic cleaning

    text = text.lower().strip()

    text = ''.join(c for c in text if c.isalnum() or

c.isspace())

    return text


sample_text = "Hello, World! This is a test."

clean_text = preprocess_text(sample_text)

tokens = tokenizer.tokenize(clean_text)

token_ids =

tokenizer.convert_tokens_to_ids(tokens)

print(token_ids)
```

1. **Custom Dataset Class**:

python

Copy code

```python
from torch.utils.data import Dataset, DataLoader


class TextDataset(Dataset):
    def __init__(self, texts, tokenizer):
        self.texts = texts
        self.tokenizer = tokenizer

    def __len__(self):
        return len(self.texts)
```

```python
    def __getitem__(self, idx):

        text = self.texts[idx]

        inputs = self.tokenizer(text,
return_tensors='pt', padding='max_length',
truncation=True, max_length=512)

        return inputs.input_ids.squeeze(),
inputs.attention_mask.squeeze()


texts = ["This is a sample text.", "Another example
sentence."]
dataset = TextDataset(texts, tokenizer)
dataloader = DataLoader(dataset, batch_size=2)

for batch in dataloader:
```

```python
    input_ids, attention_masks = batch

    print(input_ids)

    print(attention_masks)
```

2. **Loading Data**:

```python
Copy code
from datasets import load_dataset


dataset = load_dataset('wikitext', 'wikitext-2-raw-

v1')

texts = dataset['train']['text']
```

**Building LLMs from Scratch**

# Model Architecture

Building a transformer model involves several key components: embeddings, attention mechanisms, and transformer blocks.

1. **Embeddings**: Converting input tokens into dense vectors.

python

Copy code

```python
import torch.nn as nn


class Embeddings(nn.Module):
    def __init__(self, vocab_size, d_model):
        super(Embeddings, self).__init__()
```

```python
        self.embed = nn.Embedding(vocab_size, d_model)

    def forward(self, x):
        return self.embed(x)
```

2. **Attention Mechanism**: Allowing the model to focus on relevant parts of the input.

python

Copy code

```python
class SelfAttention(nn.Module):
    def __init__(self, d_model, num_heads):
        super(SelfAttention, self).__init__()
        self.num_heads = num_heads
```

```python
        self.attention =
nn.MultiheadAttention(d_model, num_heads)


    def forward(self, x):

        attn_output, _ = self.attention(x, x, x)

        return attn_output
```

3. **Transformer Blocks**: Stacking layers of attention
   and feed-forward networks.

python

Copy code

```python
class TransformerBlock(nn.Module):

    def __init__(self, d_model, num_heads,
ff_hidden_dim):

        super(TransformerBlock, self).__init__()
```

```python
        self.attention = SelfAttention(d_model,
num_heads)

        self.feed_forward = nn.Sequential(

            nn.Linear(d_model, ff_hidden_dim),

            nn.ReLU(),

            nn.Linear(ff_hidden_dim, d_model)

        )

        self.layer_norm1 = nn.LayerNorm(d_model)

        self.layer_norm2 = nn.LayerNorm(d_model)


    def forward(self, x):

        attn_output = self.attention(x)

        x = self.layer_norm1(x + attn_output)

        ff_output = self.feed_forward(x)
```

```python
        return self.layer_norm2(x + ff_output)
```

4. **Model Implementation**:

python

Copy code

```python
class TransformerModel(nn.Module):
    def __init__(self, vocab_size, d_model,
num_heads, num_layers, ff_hidden_dim):
        super(TransformerModel, self).__init__()
        self.embedding = Embeddings(vocab_size,
d_model)
        self.layers =
nn.ModuleList([TransformerBlock(d_model,
num_heads, ff_hidden_dim) for _ in
range(num_layers)])
```

```python
        self.fc_out = nn.Linear(d_model, vocab_size)


    def forward(self, x):

        x = self.embedding(x)

        for layer in self.layers:

            x = layer(x)

        return self.fc_out(x)



vocab_size = 30522  # BERT's vocabulary size

model = TransformerModel(vocab_size,

d_model=512, num_heads=8, num_layers=6,

ff_hidden_dim=2048)

input_ids = torch.randint(0, vocab_size, (32, 128))

# Batch of 32 sequences of length 128
```

```
output = model(input_ids)

print(output.shape)  # Should be (32, 128, 30522)
```

# Training Large Language Models

*Training Loop*

1. **Defining the Loss Function and Optimizer:**

   python

   Copy code

   ```python
   import torch.optim as optim

   criterion = nn.CrossEntropyLoss()

   optimizer = optim.Adam(model.parameters(),

   lr=3e-5)
   ```

2. **Training Loop:**

```python
```
Copy code

```python
num_epochs = 3
model.train()
for epoch in range(num_epochs):
    for batch in dataloader:
        input_ids, attention_masks = batch
        optimizer.zero_grad()
        outputs = model(input_ids)
        loss = criterion(outputs.view(-1, vocab_size),
input_ids.view(-1))
        loss.backward()
        optimizer.step()
    print(f"Epoch {epoch + 1}, Loss: {loss.item()}")
```

# Fine-Tuning Pretrained Models

1. **Loading Pretrained Models**:

python

Copy code

```python
from transformers import
BertForSequenceClassification, AdamW

model =
BertForSequenceClassification.from_pretrained('bert-base-uncased', num_labels=2)
optimizer = AdamW(model.parameters(), lr=2e-5)
```

2. **Fine-Tuning on a Specific Task**:

python

```
Copy code
from transformers import Trainer,
TrainingArguments

training_args = TrainingArguments(
    output_dir='./results',
    num_train_epochs=3,
    per_device_train_batch_size=8,
    per_device_eval_batch_size=8,
    warmup_steps=500,
    weight_decay=0.01,
    logging_dir='./logs',
)
```

```
trainer = Trainer(

    model=model,

    args=training_args,

    train_dataset=dataset['train'],

    eval_dataset=dataset['validation']

)


trainer.train()
```

## Evaluating LLMs

*Evaluation Metrics*

Common metrics for evaluating LLMs include:

- **Perplexity**: Measures how well a language model predicts a sample.

- **Accuracy**: For classification tasks.

- **BLEU/Rouge Scores**: For translation and summarization tasks.

*Performance Measurement*

1. **Calculating Perplexity**:

python

Copy code

```python
import math

model.eval()
with torch.no_grad():
    total_loss = 0
    for batch in dataloader:
```

```
input_ids, attention_masks = batch

outputs = model(input_ids)

loss = criterion(outputs.view(-1, vocab_size),

input_ids.view(-1))

    total_loss += loss.item()


avg_loss = total_loss / len(dataloader)

perplexity = math.exp(avg_loss)

print(f"Perplexity: {perplexity}")
```

## Deploying LLMs

*Exporting Models*

1. **Saving the Model**:

```python
python
```

Copy code

```
torch.save(model.state_dict(), 'model.pth')
```

2. **Loading the Model**:

python

Copy code

```
model = TransformerModel(vocab_size,
d_model=512, num_heads=8, num_layers=6,
ff_hidden_dim=2048)
model.load_state_dict(torch.load('model.pth'))
model.eval()
```

*Serving Models with PyTorch*

1. **Using Flask for Model Serving**:

python

```
Copy code

from flask import Flask, request, jsonify

import torch


app = Flask(__name__)


model = TransformerModel(vocab_size,

d_model=512, num_heads=8, num_layers=6,

ff_hidden_dim=2048)

model.load_state_dict(torch.load('model.pth'))

model.eval()


@app.route('/predict', methods=['POST'])

def predict():
```

```python
    data = request.json

    input_ids = torch.tensor(data['input_ids'])

    with torch.no_grad():

        outputs = model(input_ids)

    return jsonify(outputs.tolist())


if __name__ == '__main__':

    app.run()
```

## Advanced Topics

*Mixed Precision Training*

Mixed Precision Training leverages the computational

power of modern GPUs by using both 16-bit (half

precision) and 32-bit (single precision) floating point

numbers. This can significantly speed up training and reduce memory usage without sacrificing model accuracy.

**Example: Using PyTorch's torch.cuda.amp**

1. **Enable Mixed Precision Training**:

python

Copy code

```python
import torch

from torch.cuda.amp import autocast, GradScaler


scaler = GradScaler()


for epoch in range(num_epochs):
```

```
model.train()

for input_ids, attention_masks in dataloader:

    optimizer.zero_grad()

    with autocast():

        outputs = model(input_ids)

        loss = criterion(outputs.view(-1, vocab_size),

input_ids.view(-1))

    scaler.scale(loss).backward()

    scaler.step(optimizer)

    scaler.update()
```

**Use Cases**:

- **Training Large Models**: Reduces the memory

  footprint, allowing for larger batch sizes or deeper

  models.

- **Speed Optimization**: Speeds up training by utilizing Tensor Cores on Nvidia GPUs.

*Distributed Training*

Distributed training allows you to train large models across multiple GPUs or even multiple machines, significantly reducing training time.

**Example: Using PyTorch's torch.nn.DataParallel and torch.distributed**

1. **Single-Machine Multi-GPU Training**:

python

Copy code

```
import torch

import torch.nn as nn
```

```python
import torch.optim as optim

from torch.utils.data import DataLoader


# Model

model =

nn.DataParallel(TransformerModel(vocab_size,

d_model=512, num_heads=8, num_layers=6,

ff_hidden_dim=2048)).cuda()


# Optimizer and Criterion

optimizer = optim.Adam(model.parameters(),

lr=3e-5)

criterion = nn.CrossEntropyLoss()
```

```python
# Training Loop

for epoch in range(num_epochs):

    model.train()

    for input_ids, attention_masks in dataloader:

        input_ids, attention_masks = input_ids.cuda(), attention_masks.cuda()

        optimizer.zero_grad()

        outputs = model(input_ids)

        loss = criterion(outputs.view(-1, vocab_size), input_ids.view(-1))

        loss.backward()

        optimizer.step()
```

## 2. Multi-Machine Distributed Training:

python

```
Copy code

import torch.distributed as dist

from torch.nn.parallel import

DistributedDataParallel as DDP


def setup(rank, world_size):
    dist.init_process_group("nccl", rank=rank,
world_size=world_size)


def cleanup():
    dist.destroy_process_group()


def train(rank, world_size):
    setup(rank, world_size)
```

```python
    model = TransformerModel(vocab_size,
d_model=512, num_heads=8, num_layers=6,
ff_hidden_dim=2048).cuda(rank)
    ddp_model = DDP(model, device_ids=[rank])
    optimizer =
optim.Adam(ddp_model.parameters(), lr=3e-5)
    criterion = nn.CrossEntropyLoss()


    for epoch in range(num_epochs):
        ddp_model.train()
        for input_ids, attention_masks in dataloader:
            input_ids, attention_masks =
input_ids.cuda(rank), attention_masks.cuda(rank)
            optimizer.zero_grad()
```

```
        outputs = ddp_model(input_ids)

        loss = criterion(outputs.view(-1, vocab_size),

input_ids.view(-1))

        loss.backward()

        optimizer.step()


    cleanup()


world_size = 2  # Number of GPUs

mp.spawn(train, args=(world_size,),

nprocs=world_size, join=True)
```

**Use Cases**:

- **Training Large Datasets**: Efficiently processes large

  datasets by distributing the load.

- **Faster Training**: Reduces training time for large models.

*Handling Large-Scale Data*

Handling large-scale data involves efficient data loading, preprocessing, and augmentation to ensure smooth and fast training.

**Example: Using PyTorch's DataLoader and Dataset**

1. **Creating a Custom Dataset**:

python

Copy code

```python
import torch
from torch.utils.data import Dataset, DataLoader
```

```python
class LargeTextDataset(Dataset):

    def __init__(self, file_path, tokenizer,
max_length=512):

        self.file_path = file_path

        self.tokenizer = tokenizer

        self.max_length = max_length

        self.data = self.load_data()


    def load_data(self):
        with open(self.file_path, 'r') as f:

            return f.readlines()


    def __len__(self):

        return len(self.data)
```

```python
    def __getitem__(self, idx):

        text = self.data[idx]

        inputs = self.tokenizer(text,
return_tensors='pt', padding='max_length',
truncation=True, max_length=self.max_length)

        return inputs.input_ids.squeeze(),
inputs.attention_mask.squeeze()


tokenizer = BertTokenizer.from_pretrained('bert-
base-uncased')
dataset = LargeTextDataset('large_text_corpus.txt',
tokenizer)
```

```
dataloader = DataLoader(dataset, batch_size=8,

num_workers=4)
```

**Use Cases**:

- **Big Data**: Efficiently handling large volumes of text data.

- **Optimized Data Loading**: Faster data loading and preprocessing for high throughput.

*Model Compression Techniques*

Model compression techniques help in deploying LLMs on resource-constrained devices by reducing model size and inference time.

**Example: Using Quantization and Pruning in Py

Torch**

# 1. Quantization:

python

Copy code

```python
import torch

from torch.quantization import quantize_dynamic


# Load the pretrained model

model = torch.load('model.pth')


# Apply dynamic quantization

quantized_model = quantize_dynamic(model,

{torch.nn.Linear}, dtype=torch.qint8)


# Save the quantized model
```

```
torch.save(quantized_model,
'quantized_model.pth')
```

2. **Pruning**:

```python
Copy code
import torch
import torch.nn.utils.prune as prune


# Define the model
model = TransformerModel(vocab_size,
d_model=512, num_heads=8, num_layers=6,
ff_hidden_dim=2048)


# Apply pruning to the linear layers
```

```python
for name, module in model.named_modules():

    if isinstance(module, torch.nn.Linear):

        prune.l1_unstructured(module,

name='weight', amount=0.4)

        prune.remove(module, 'weight')


# Save the pruned model

torch.save(model.state_dict(), 'pruned_model.pth')
```

**Use Cases**:

- **Edge Deployment**: Deploying models on mobile or IoT devices.

- **Reduced Inference Time**: Faster model inference for real-time applications.

# Case Studies and Applications

*Practical Examples and Use Cases*

1. **Chatbot Development**:

   - **Goal**: Create a chatbot that can handle customer service queries.

   - **Implementation**: Fine-tune a pretrained GPT model on customer service conversations.

   - **Code**:

   python

   Copy code

   ```
   from transformers import GPT2LMHeadModel,
   GPT2Tokenizer
   ```

```python
model_name = 'gpt2-medium'

tokenizer =
GPT2Tokenizer.from_pretrained(model_name)

model =
GPT2LMHeadModel.from_pretrained(model_
name)


# Fine-tuning on custom dataset (assume
'train_dataset' is already prepared)

from transformers import Trainer,
TrainingArguments

training_args = TrainingArguments(
    output_dir='./results',
```

```python
    num_train_epochs=3,

    per_device_train_batch_size=8,

    per_device_eval_batch_size=8,

    warmup_steps=500,

    weight_decay=0.01,

    logging_dir='./logs',
)


trainer = Trainer(

    model=model,

    args=training_args,

    train_dataset=train_dataset,

    eval_dataset=eval_dataset
)
```

```
trainer.train()
```

## 2. Sentiment Analysis:

- **Goal**: Classify customer reviews as positive or negative.

- **Implementation**: Fine-tune a BERT model on a labeled sentiment dataset.

- **Code**:

python

Copy code

```
from transformers import
BertForSequenceClassification, BertTokenizer,
Trainer, TrainingArguments
```

```python
model_name = 'bert-base-uncased'

tokenizer = BertTokenizer.from_pretrained(model_name)

model = BertForSequenceClassification.from_pretrained(model_name, num_labels=2)


# Prepare the dataset
from datasets import load_dataset


dataset = load_dataset('imdb')
train_dataset = dataset['train']
eval_dataset = dataset['test']
```

```python
# Fine-tuning

training_args = TrainingArguments(

    output_dir='./results',

    num_train_epochs=3,

    per_device_train_batch_size=8,

    per_device_eval_batch_size=8,

    warmup_steps=500,

    weight_decay=0.01,

    logging_dir='./logs',

)


trainer = Trainer(

    model=model,

    args=training_args,
```

```
    train_dataset=train_dataset,

    eval_dataset=eval_dataset

)



trainer.train()
```

*Success Stories*

1. **OpenAI GPT-3**:

    ○ **Achievement**: Developed one of the largest
    and most powerful language models.

    ○ **Impact**: Enabled various applications, from
    creative writing and programming assistance
    to generating human-like text.

- Key Points: Utilized extensive computational resources, mixed precision training, and innovative model architecture.

2. **Google BERT**:

   - **Achievement**: Improved performance on numerous NLP tasks and set new benchmarks.

   - **Impact**: Enhanced search engine understanding and various NLP applications.

   - **Key Points**: Introduced the transformer architecture and the concept of bidirectional training.

## Troubleshooting and Best Practices

1. **Out of Memory Errors**:

   ○ **Solution**: Reduce batch size, use gradient accumulation, or enable mixed precision training.

   ○ **Example**:

   python

   Copy code

   ```
   from torch.cuda.amp import autocast, GradScaler

   scaler = GradScaler()

   for epoch in range(num_epochs):
   ```

```
model.train()

for input_ids, attention_masks in

dataloader:

    optimizer.zero_grad()

    with autocast():

        outputs = model(input_ids)

        loss = criterion(outputs.view(-1,

vocab_size), input_ids.view(-1))

    scaler.scale(loss).backward()

    scaler.step(optimizer)

    scaler.update()
```

2. **Slow Training**:

- ○ **Solution**: Use efficient data loaders, enable mixed precision training, or distribute training across multiple GPUs.

- ○ **Example**:

python

Copy code

```
from torch.utils.data import DataLoader


dataloader = DataLoader(dataset,
batch_size=8, num_workers=4)
```

3. **Convergence Issues**:

- ○ **Solution**: Check data preprocessing, adjust learning rate, use learning rate schedulers, or try different optimization algorithms.

- **Example**:

python

Copy code

```python
from torch.optim.lr_scheduler import StepLR


optimizer = optim.Adam(model.parameters(), lr=3e-5)
scheduler = StepLR(optimizer, step_size=1, gamma=0.1)


for epoch in range(num_epochs):
    model.train()
    for input_ids, attention_masks in dataloader:
```

```
optimizer.zero_grad()

outputs = model(input_ids)

loss = criterion(outputs.view(-1,

vocab_size), input_ids.view(-1))

loss.backward()

optimizer.step()

scheduler.step()
```

*Tips for Efficient Training and Deployment*

1. **Batch Size and Learning Rate**:

    ○ Adjust batch size and learning rate to balance

    convergence speed and stability.

    ○ Use learning rate schedulers to adapt the

    learning rate during training.

2. **Early Stopping**:

- Monitor validation loss and implement early stopping to prevent overfitting.

- **Example:**

python

Copy code

```python
from torch.utils.data import DataLoader


dataloader = DataLoader(dataset, batch_size=8, num_workers=4)


best_val_loss = float('inf')

patience = 2

trigger_times = 0
```

```python
for epoch in range(num_epochs):

    model.train()

    for input_ids, attention_masks in
dataloader:

        optimizer.zero_grad()

        outputs = model(input_ids)

        loss = criterion(outputs.view(-1,
vocab_size), input_ids.view(-1))

        loss.backward()

        optimizer.step()


    # Validation phase

    model.eval()

    val_loss = 0
```

```python
with torch.no_grad():

    for input_ids, attention_masks in
val_dataloader:

        outputs = model(input_ids)

        val_loss += criterion(outputs.view(-1,
vocab_size), input_ids.view(-1)).item()

    val_loss /= len(val_dataloader)


    if val_loss < best_val_loss:

        best_val_loss = val_loss

        trigger_times = 0

    else:

        trigger_times += 1

        if trigger_times >= patience:
```

```
        print("Early stopping triggered.")

        break
```

3. **Efficient Data Loading**:

   ○ Use multiple workers for data loading to speed up the data pipeline.

   ○ **Example**:

   python

   Copy code

   ```
   dataloader = DataLoader(dataset,
   batch_size=8, num_workers=4)
   ```

4. **Model Checkpointing**:

- Save model checkpoints during training to prevent data loss and enable resuming training.

- **Example**:

python

Copy code

```
torch.save(model.state_dict(),
'model_checkpoint.pth')
```